MAGED PORTRAIT
OF THE POET
AS AN ENGINEER
ZAHER

2009 : PRESSED WAFER : BOSTON, MASS.

*type*slowly designed

Printed by Cushing-Malloy, Inc.
    on Glatfelter Natures Recycled paper

The author would like to thank the editors of the following
magazines, where some of the poems of this book were
originally published: *Alice Blue Review, Bedazzler, Columbia
Poetry Review, Cranky, Exquisite Corpse, Golden Handcuff
Review, Jacket, New American Writing, Ribot, Tinfish, Weird
deer,* and *West Coast Line.*

The author would also like to thank Chris Dusterhoff for his
thorough review of the manuscript.

First printing in 2009

ISBN 978-0-9824100-1-1

Pressed Wafer/ 9 Columbus Square / Boston, Mass. 02116

pressed-wafer.blogspot.com

CONTENTS

Poems 2000 – 2005

Poems 2005 – 2007

For the Arabic language

And for Marcel, Amal, Daniel, and Noel

Poems 2000 – 2005

The Inferno

At lunchtime, we took our khaki pants, meeting agendas and went there, the fourth circle of hell, by the espresso machine. I saw him, with plastic tubes coming out of his body, my drinking buddy, the one who told me that I can be romantic, trustful, and still practice safe sex. Dante was there too, sipping bad wine and flirting with the girls in the massage lounge. He told me: Beatrice was a mid-life crisis thing, a career opportunity, and when the damn paparazzi surrounded the Ritz he smelled her death in the eyes of the bell captain. I asked: master, master, is Barry White a great romantic? Which should I work for: startups or established? Which is more truthful: the DOW or the NASDAQ? He looked into my tearful eyes and said: Son, search inside thyself. The Trojan War is just a myth. IPO's are your best bet. Don't search for Beatrice, and don't repeat my mistakes: Whenever you buy a pack of cigarettes ask not for one, but two sets of matches. Your friend was right: you can be romantic, trustful, and still practice safe sex.

Blood economic

Pass the light twice
      before noon
            & hit your head
                  against the city map

Your mouth shall bleed
      while going down
            on a strange woman

Calm her. Tell her it is the magnetic fields of her dreams.
Bring a vector calculus book and draw her smile. She
will think you are romantic and drink your Christian
blood while erasing all the messages from your answering
machine.

For the love of ideology

I dreamt of chairman Mao jumping between skyscrapers. NY cops were after him. He told me that he never agreed on the separation of the spice girls. I found myself screaming: "I LOVE CHAIRMAN MAO. I LOVE CHAIRMAN MAO." He taught me how to use chopsticks and stole me watermelons in his truck. He told me that I don't need flowers to fall in love. Chairman Mao never killed the people he disagreed with; they volunteered their death.

The heavy window

The heavy window is covered with an outdated map. These are the territories that postmen used to hide in from their daily routine. Home is not beyond this fallen tent: you need to distill it from national pride & other languages. There is no ocean here — only bankrupt fountains, outdated concerns, and the green shadow of a Marxist drag queen hiding in the proletariat long strike. Expectedly, I am nostalgic for Cairo streets, my friends lousy driving records, & to a late night cab ride into early Christianity.

Detachment

the brown passengers
             of the 747
                          died

while in a strip mall
             shopping
                          for an apocalypse

believe in cucumber (or ezra pound)

detachments

door knobs by the dozen

I am saving your name for a
happy ending

Love letters from the middle class

..

Yeah, me too, I love you. Sorry for the dramatic title. I am working 9-7. It's a reality show out here: magic princesses in BMW's will cut your throat for a dollar, but it's also so lovely to have free soda all day.

I miss you
love, sarah

Yo Sarah — have you found the never never home of your dreams yet?

I hate civilization sometimes, say hi to your boyfriend — I miss him too.

most love,
ramy

Ramy, John says "Hi." we went to a small nightmare
yesterday and swam with the ducks. It was okay.

I miss you too. And by the way, how's corporate America
treating you?

Have you received the Baudelaire book I sent?
send me a poem please

love, sarah

I found a magic carpet yesterday and flew east but you
were busy   so I spent the rest of the night in a tuxedo
pretending that money doesn't matter, and bought you
some west coast wine —

sorry about the poem   I am not writing much lately

ramy

damn it — why do you always have to be so tragic? — got the pictures you sent. shave your beard.

love, sarah

Sarah, back to square one (I used to call it loneliness, now it feels great) come over next time you're in town. I gave up on casual sex, but a threesome isn't such a bad idea. or is it?

love, ramy

Ramy, yes, it's a bad idea, but an orgasm may help you get real. I am thinking I will come with the butterflies and we can torture each other kindly

love, sarah

. . .

Desert prayers

The Christian monks of the Egyptian desert are flawless. They are there for no apparent reason. Beautiful women come to their dreams and strangle them or take them on short trips in fearful cities. The deeply troubled of them are saints and they usually make it to the next world without psychiatrists. They are praying for me so I may overcome happiness. & I think of them & their black clothes & I — too — pray for them & ask for a second chance in the Egyptian desert. But I am not sure about living without skin or fingers. So don't turn the light on yet & let me give it one more shot using candles — just wait & pray — & I promise that I won't be happy.

Forget the bus take the train

as a globalization effect the ku klux klan are playing reggae
in the background   go hungry for a week to pass the
Christian values test   fuck assimilation and non-arranged
marriages   this is ambition: fallen bodies lose their
inhibition when they hit the ground   violate me not my
boundaries and give the suburbs another shot: motorcycle
riding classes for the middle class   mathematicians are
seldom wrong   conclusion: mathematics is superior to
other sciences   can we have sex now please   I will leave
no marks on your body   I promise

I, Karl Marx, declare my
inner contradictions

Variation – 1
I, Karl Marx, remember that my comrades — whom
we shared together the cigarettes, the whiskey and the
class struggle — had left me to my thoughts. I turned to
God: Father, father, why have you left me? The Roman
counselor refused to offer me the plea-bargain and drank
my blood with the central committee. I told him, you
shall see me again, I shall resurrect in the WTO protest,
I will be an angry woman with pink hair, and when the
city turns republican, I shall offer my body and blood to
the last tear gas bomb holder. He shall kiss me on the lips
and they will crucify me again.

Variation – 2
I, Karl Marx, was not with the Russian troops in Prague.
These were not my pictures on the tanks. I was not the
grand inquisitor of Spain. I did not order the burn of the
Jews, the Heretics, to protect the true belief in proletarian
values.

I, Karl Marx, am a descendant of the Pharaohs, but in
case any of my grandmothers fucked a Greek, an Arab,
a Persian, or a Turk, I might not be able to guarantee my
ethnic purity.

Her

don't let that white space scare you —
       even the decadence of artists

your throat is clogged
with her name
you fall in love with the idea of her
or the reality of her dualities

you tell her:
       I am from far beyond your skies

you tell her:
       they are not kind here nor there

& you tell her that you will project your thoughts of
ideal love on her & that you will overload her voice with
meanings — then you wait for her to touch you or leave
forever — & silently you take the far corner of the church
& pray that she would stay

Strangers in the night

Help me represent my desire
in formal decrees.   And help me handle
this noise's supreme arrogance like a man
who has proper dreadlock fantasies
and who is metaphysically aware
— as he should be — of America
dancing on a Thursday night
or contemplating spending
this disastrous winter without
getting fascinated by anything
other than this near-by Internet café
providing access to quick comrades.

Cyber-proletariat of the world, chat freely.
But let us also remember that these words
have no life in themselves.
Well, I was too drunk to unhook her bra
but we fucked anyway.

Love letter

Today I enjoyed waking up with you
and watching your first sentiments,
before we started building
the corners of our sentences
to isolate each other.
Before we started gazing
at the empty part of the room
that defied both decoration and intimacy.
This part of the room
where yesterday's condom rests
and acts as a symbol of something.

The city with round dining tables

I thought then that I need better nightmares. Nightmares that reflect my inner conflicts. Take for example, a nightmare about women in men's clothes ordering take out in a Chinese restaurant. Imagine the insights such a dream could tell me about myself.

I knew that I have (sic) to ask for forgiveness, but I was not sure from whom: As a start I excluded Michelangelo's saints. This fracture started from the heart and went all the way to the concrete wall. In the middle of the foggy streets I called for Rimbaud. I told him: exile is a sexual position. He disagreed: exile is a state of betrayal, and at night you don't have the right to look yourself in the mirror.

Fresh memory

I will always open the car door for you, just don't damage me with your eyes or your wet fingers. I am in this country without memories and I would like to keep it that way for a while.

What's sex got to do with memories? This is how sentimental I can be without you, so let us go to Mexico & get a divorce. Meanwhile we could fuck other people on the side to test the common theory of true love.

Daniel is an elephant

Clare is chasing dreamy firemen in my dream.
No, this was Jackie's dream — the fire is real though —
I am in Atlanta, teaching Daniel his first Arabic poetry line:
"al-khailo wal-lailo wal-baidae taarefonee"
Daniel puts a shoestring in his mouth
and tells me that he is an elephant
and I am rearranging the animal's taxonomy for him.
Earlier today, I emailed Heather about
the poet-as-a-fish: "Ignore my falling in love with you,
I ran out of better things to do,
so please disregard my overt compliments,
and continue being your charming self"

Mohamed tells me that I am obsessed
with language and that he likes my poems
best when I am falling in or out of love.
I am trying to convince him that God
lives within the torques of syntax: "God
is form, love is the content or whatever"
        Mohamed is leaving for Cairo in two weeks,
        so we cut out the poetics,
        and finish our beers.

Forking it

Will come, signaling, a dream's end
stuttering, off-beat, buy your
       shadows again, the light often
       blends with syntax.

That stream, forked, in big cars
how amusing
to walk, next to your tongue,
with a floating compass
looking for a harbor.

That pen is your distance,

I am your left shoulder. Do not wake me up —
the architect will testify, tomorrow,
against my dream.

Pet the tip of the wave, and hope
that your printed directions
are accurate.

21st century Bellevue

21st century Bellevue: a tall woman with dark skin assumes that I am her lover. Picks a wedding day & tells me: no sex for now.

There is inevitability in what she does. She tells me: take your fear of sea lions elsewhere. Screams: bring me happiness. In the parking spot designated for lovers, I touch my knee and tell her: we are fucked: nuclear power, ethnic hate.

She stands there, you know, every passerby is a potential sperm donor. She cries: love me but don't love my body. Suddenly, I remembered the dry blood from the last night accident on I-5, the tortured flesh of middle-eastern political prisoners, and Prague. Prague, your women out drink me. Awkwardness. The continuation of a thought that was never fully formed: your dreams, ah, your dreams are not choreographed appropriately, let someone else decide.

This is not an angry poem

In the process of facing the world he used to carry a picture of his dentist in his wallet. Which helped shaping his political views: The class struggle is over, we could not make the playoffs. We need a better head coach next year. Trotsky is too left. Stalin is too nice. They abandoned their truck to his backyard and bad mouthed the quality of his prisons.

He has the eye color of my uncle, and her footsteps. I have to go back or lose my accent forever. You have to stop fucking around with your identity, you are what you were born into since there is no room for expansion in the fiscal report. Just shut up and believe the goddamn motherfuckers who lied to her about the health insurance coverage, or about the proper time to get off the pills so we can fuck while concentrating on not bringing more people to this world.

The poet and the city are
extensions of each other

But cities are promiscuous, so here I am
saving my best desires for the next world: one last
cultural project to flatten the hierarchies of angels.

Next to you in the movie theater, I believed that
we had the clouds all for ourselves,
although in the cheap tavern, when I pressed the
ice cube to your lips, you closed your eyes
and it started raining outside.

A trap for St. Augustine

We learn about madness: about words walking as ghosts.
The choice of verb tense will control your shadows and the
extent of what you can promise your family. Weekend sex
will not turn into geography, tell them that, and tell them
that you are dead to the world, Augustine, and go on the
wagon.

But remember that the two paths are not as parallel as you
think. So spread the dense metaphor over multiple pages.
(We might finally convince someone of heaven.)

A dream of graduate school

you will eventually learn not to care about the differences
between alligators & crocodiles   but Jesus!   they are
everywhere we will have to evacuate our cul-de-sac & act
as pedestrians whom are evacuated from their cul-de-sac

(he is not a fag motherfuckers: he is a transsexual & you
have no idea how it feels living in a body that mismatches
your desires)

+ there are rabbits all over the place?
+ pack them with you.   it is one hour past our
  time to go

Garrison for hairdressers

garrison for hairdressers   (this city is or will be) but
think of that as a ramification   dear editor, he was at
least earnest while getting a blowjob in the parking garage
it was the bridesmaid's idea   so you can't really call it
plagiarism   the speedometer is bounded by the idea of
measurement   hence, we think of gravity as a form of
sound & abandon it for the silence of road signs   nothing
will prevent me from that desire   neither the age difference
nor the bad haircut

There is always a starting point

there is always a starting point, then a runway with pictures
from back-ordered issues of the *Times*. you jumped two
steps at a time & lost all your religious friends, but you will
still be able to save the fire extinguisher & think that you
don't have an imagination problem (& that the question of
closed systems boils down to the accuracy of the scientist's
assumptions).

you said that you can always invent the concept of oceans
& console the sad seamen (with pictures of Hemingway
in their pockets) who are there searching for the platform.
you forgot that the battery is almost dead & the couch is
wet — and the only proper thing to do is drown.

Naming them

we shall forgive infinity & go down the winter path to deserted train stations & use 7-11 phone cards to talk to God in San Francisco & we will stop believing.

& in surgeries, we will think of alternative medicine, of heaven or hell, & of train station operators losing their jobs because of God or market dynamics.

& we will feel strong about everything — but nothing will change the inevitability of empty train stations or the mercy of doctors

but can we really merge these two worlds with one airplane trip?

> I promise
> I will name my feelings

A love song for Paris Hilton

Facing death we stick to our pretentiousness: some symbolism, some constructivism, and a tad bit of reality. How did we end up in an affair with syntax? First we did identity politics in the suburbs, where we found out that this is the wireless age and settled for these semi-dorky conversations about content vs. form.

We went to the lecture hall full of hope: theory is practice. Yet old school critics & experimental poets were roaming the cyber-space for a good fuck: alas, we were left in chat rooms like inferior angels.

Self-hate is an expensive skill: indoor sunglasses, the same set of pick-up lines & voilà: we got the fashion industry folks cornered on the dance floor & we threw a good punch or two before the music ended.

So Paris, come hither to the cyber-ghetto of experimental poets. The night is freckled with its stars but my language is yours, dear; my dear language is dearly yours.

Poems 2005 – 2007

My software mission

1

A message from your dept. store manager:
"Imagine staying as one person after all this fiction"

Cultural diversity a standard ritual:
clap twice then take off your clothes;
the media already created a gap
to enable you to meet your abstract other
devouring a cab seat in the suburbs

where we have it all: the theory, its
supporting documents, and a gentle freak show
bringing democracy to them
one dead Arab at a time.

Why should I give up my benign neurosis?
You stick to the legal definition of innocence
and leave me the task of creating memories:
internet   volleyball   a quick cause

The next show involves silence
and self-stripping utterance.
But all they had is one air-hockey table
which turned our lives into a background
for the traffic conditions.

The suede jacket will eventually
play an important role
as we're suddenly asleep on the dance floor
meanwhile the immense dream of lust
that surrounded us
has no power.

Which is not the same as being free
from theory's nagging despair
we owe our hunger to the map's persistence
(which didn't prevent us from participating
in inventing new terminologies)

This was where rigor met cuteness
and told bedtime stories all morning.
Basically, we were overwhelmed with symbols
so we escaped from the city's downtown
where I bought my first dictionary
and looked up half the words in fear
of never knowing the other half.

The neon of the same city carried me —
like a lame prophet — to its outstanding coffee shops.

Yes, mine is a standard story of time spent the
worst way. Although theory books
gave me a reason to be happy.

Later I grew a beard and wept for
all the surplus value generated over history.

How old was this sadness I rescued
and held onto despite my formal hallucinations?

The poet's business is to be surrounded by death
instead of local politicians.

New Year's resolutions: to have a coherent story
and spend time with gym rats
who possess the gentleness of statisticians
then reevaluate this excellent status-quo
with well-rested imagination.

Expect the report on recycled paper:
form was our obvious truth
as we navigated the tight schedule
to learn about Sinbad's obsessive journey
in order to get back the severed head of the prophet

We didn't leave the town before mastering its rhythm.

Yesterday the wall buried us swimming
between two violent streams of jelly beans.

I was hoping to see you tonight
in one of these marginalized coffee shops
but the ocean wave took the night shift
and participated in the music sales:
trains of hands and shoulders,
the body easily dismantled
so there was little we can do about our desires.

We were influenced by a collage
of weeping space travelers.

Take your skull out of the equation
as you're growing your nails
to defend the campus' policemen.

2

The phonemes we used to leave voice
messages showed up first in childhood
before we burned our limited body language
in a copy of the apocalypse
(the pure version that follows each death)

All the symptoms of mysticism
were lost under the city's delightful rain
and in the terrific tragedy of realizing (or not)
that the love that looms like l=o=v=e
looms only in my software mission
and the cute emergencies
of a stranger extrapolating
his jealousy of the natives
and prompting himself to save his secular freedom
with vodka martinis.

Tormented with his elaborate blog
the space creatures orbit

his busted metaphysical quest:
in the right frame of mind
I would be falling on your little feet
— Berryman style —
but my worst fear is heaven:
its laminated layers
and the isolation of the dreams that lead to it.

Looking from these irregular windows
lead to my voyeurism.

Yet, I saved the dress code for the future engineers
who paid for hope in cash (and sometimes in songs)
but would it help if they revoked your driving privilege?

It's still a long shot to find love
while playing a secondary role in the script.

3

Roaming in a body bag of Cartesian illusions,
what a strange choice of vacation spots?

I rubbed the moon with my forehead first
then threw charcoal at the town's kids.
I did it twice.

This was at one end of the moment
in the squash court: Canadians and Pakistanis
transforming their lust for their loved ones
into backhand shots.

Think of an indie movie,
and when asked for a grand story,
answer: "expat lyrics on foam."

I am the keeper of all good starts
and my neighbor's colloquial diaspora
promoting his urban dream of missed prayers.

Seattle fleece jacket bohemia town
I dream. My dream is full of khakis
and yes, I did it for love.
I did it unexpectedly out of love.

Sending my letters using liquid stamps
the middleman is trapped
in his consistency of thought
(his task was not as sexy.)

So, Dr. Williams, I'm still operating in ideas.
For example, the space won't swallow
the concrete pages of the neighborhood.

They blew up the opposition leader in the morning,
meanwhile the vendors tracked the honest conspiracy.

(a sudden poem for Henry Michaux)
Given the same gestures we arrived at different conclusions.
You kissed my girl twice you bastard
but even when you frighten me
we still break bread in the European Union's halls
and ask poets to love unconditionally
and use words as sex toys, so the pressure
of bodies on other bodies seems appropriate.

But Henry, fuck it man, all the barbarians
are on coffee breaks
meanwhile, the wave is holding its trendy shirt
and the unbuttoned button of the ant farm future.

The sea re-structured its public image
and left me with an orange to peel
and a desperate bottom line of reason.

Exercising my semantic rights, I know
something will eventually never happen.

Yet be careful buddy, we stayed in the thick traffic
waiting for a new future with its in-depth manual
about the merits of describing sanity
without the silliness of memories creeping up.

I can prove that there is a correlation between
the shape of winter and our massive hopelessness,
so I keep playing it safe and disregard the traffic
in order to keep the pictures of my loved ones near.

In my backup plan the body disintegrates

The great memo maker notebook:
+   Minimize contact with your environment.
+   Pick an alliance with the night; the morning is safe by
        definition.
+   Prepare for the urban scene: a body is a pre-condition
        for lust.

The robots mark the street as if we aren't going anywhere
and all the kissing business is not just a façade.
Our designated driver took notes while alive
but the narrator is the one who was given immunity
for keeping a precise offset from reality
while building a prayer from to-do lists.

Now that we satisfied the god of statistics
we promise we will protect your privacy,
and give you back your exact change.

I'm interested in the blame
language of wine lists

I'm interested in the blame language of wine lists
I'm interested in your sweat shops
And the random patterns of luxury they offer me
All my lovers are gathered in a kitchen
How is your cave's electricity, dear lovers?
Meaning still moves me, and my poems are still largely
        about sex
And I still expect the bridge to alert the water it guards
        from the garbage of the passengers
Given all the torture scenes, my pretend spirit is low
There are times where we should order a side salad instead
— it is called responsibility
The poets I know travel a lot to renew their licenses and stuff
One of them carried a slab and hit the foreman
It was his tough guy fantasy
Except that he should have never tried to time the market
We blasted through the first phase of the project
With all our met & unmet needs
The market gave us technology but kept us in the lab
We are the working lab rats escaping poverty, and we're
        fucked
But Multimedia helped heal our feelings
Yet we're still on our toes: productive work force
Listening to the sins of existence: I will deploy
My cognitive model daily in your service, my dear CEO

Forgive all these insider traders father for they know shit
Send your report to the translation committee instead
They will save you from obscurity when
Diplomacy takes a dive, and as we rise in the streets
To solve family disputes in the same torture rooms
The academics suggested we use for Arabs
The same academics who rewrote the history of ideas and
        explained:
Let us enjoy the mathematical constraints free market offers
Give me your big colorful shirt and I will walk around naked
Surrounded by fiscal responsibilities I will look so square
Behind these glasses I will nest your cut throat monsters
And suck your big nipples for less than ten thousand dollars
I will accept your street musicians as my brothers and sisters
And will passionately love your useless radicals — no one
        in particular
I will love the idea of walking this strip drunk:
Astounding train stations and bus stops
One more love lost for the day
Six more hours and we will send the helicopters
To breathe over your friend's neck
Please abridge your rumors and let it pass as small talk
No more demanding empirical evidence, a theoretical one
        should suffice
This particular cuisine is abstracted
She was a small town woman at heart yet with a fully
        developed death drive

Rented luxuries

(made out of collapsing thoughts)

phase i

in an ahead closet, a warning:
ideologies are funny this way

and it will cost dearly to give into reason
without at least a hug
but across the borders
syntax can order things
except this permanent thread:
forgettable like a movie

overwhelmed with passengers' screams
the experts stepped in: "you are wrong.
make a quick phone call and leave"

the fireplace isn't a secret
so come at 5:15
it is not just beach volleyball
it is a state of heightened awareness

kissing in the bar — in essence — is a Brechtian scene
backed up with menu items
but wait for God before drinking
it is a spot where early death is safe and guaranteed

"please don't bend your gender"
the body might accumulate opposite desires
oh carpenters and locksmiths
we often locked ourselves outside
hoping for your sympathy

premium gravity:
we discovered that we owe batman everything
they sent someone down the pipes to talk
about love "hello, it has been a wonderful
journey to the middle of the pacific and back"
yet after a right turn I am faced with the sun:
critical and made exclusively out of thoughts
and of giant proportions like any good pizza

recall the impairment from hunger
this isn't a lovely world
but I do still wish for a tree
to sleep under where apples
fall without gravity's tireless drama

he wouldn't wake up earlier
to think of the reflection
of things on other things

so — in a theatrical move — he
declared a final belief system
and said that he wanted us to be happy
he was taking every opportunity to move
slower than his own thoughts

who then opened
the construction site
and found his identity in it?

the town is well dressed
but things will shift
to complete a market cycle

being an arab
the field opens
for a game of hide-n-seek
identity is imposed or constructed or both
and is always hidden under a wave of exotic
killing   a measure democracies use against
their natural enemies   but
what is the order things should vanish in?
it was an explosion in the traditional
sense of the word:
the body positioned next to a limited supply of reality

the novel's voice
an animation movie
made out of pay stubs

to ignite a romantic whole
in case we fall behind the market
to the extent of feeling proud
of this mom and pop restaurant
at the edge of capitalism

telling of the discontinuity
of lovers — their lack of granularity
their parallelism to clouds
nurturing a body eating itself
avoiding popcorn and movies
and focusing on the fiscal year's campaign:
boring music in exciting spiritual venues

would you leave it dangling
from the last playoffs
God watched instead of taking
care of us? — these were the days
when we aimed for better
technology and made it our passion
then it rained in some other story
and we told the business people
"this is a crazy dream
even if it started in childhood
as a way to understand the
structure of things"
facing a square parking lot,
the self identifies
with the tight spaces between

the cars and wonders
at which point the surroundings
became a necessity
for the systematic
production of sentiments
the neon of things too
is a form of textual pleasure
bless this breadth we came to
for happiness: immigrants, engineers,
and occasional folk
singers we — it's a kind landscape
so we were told, yet
quantity matters too: the pyramids,
cotton candy

dialogue doesn't preclude assassinations
reverting fate using digital photography

the family reunion was interrupted
when she asked for her father
the cry that took her over
the illusive intellect her future lovers
will ignore — the lovely path the world
will offer to her wounds
and the boy who will sing to her:
"touch this river
touch it twice
it is an abusive landscape
the way there is always a mountain
to leave behind"

I know that I missed the point
here is my ride, and here is
an average joke before leaving
for civilization wearing this stupid costume
a description of heaven may follow
traveling solo with hope carried underwater

there will be workshops
and we will talk about building a great ithaca!
in our way to ithaca
we will have at least one
dinner with the industry leaders

market share (again)
waiting gets ugly but it is exactly as advertised:

my distance from cordova
is collage material
plan b is suppressing emotional availability

the software boys and the gangsters are hitting
the same strip joint tonight
and they lived happily in the aftermath of it
but without promising much to the rest of us

for the second day in a row, he had difficulties
hiding being a sex symbol: window or aisle?
the rest is kinda irrelevant
given all the underground you can

zip through for the buck
it took a full team of designers and theorists
an eternity to drag our global village to listen to
the spokesman announcing a highway of company logos

during the process of building software
I learned about my desire
and it is not pretty
all portable devices are
to be disabled — symmetry is
out of style — which seemed to be something
everybody else knew
it is radical to trust your engine
outside its cultural context
but it won't kill you any slower though to think otherwise
oh, honey, the self is a historical
construction guarded by floating SUVs
and the asymptotic game of death
plastics, metals with spiritual leanings that is wrecked
with thunderstorms: order matters
so I am lost unless instructed otherwise

the east coast: ménage á trois
converting the new jersey turnpike
into words: although nothing is like family
oh, new york, what if I have more poetic
response to jersey? the schizophrenic existence
of immigrant families played against despairingly
long commutes

on top of the empire state building
on a monday morning
the jersey turnpike is a space of tears:
hello daniel, it is dad here

read it like an escape plan
or like a roadmap of
finger pointing techniques
a terrific indictment was
over heard — for once —
we — too — are exploitable
which is organization theory at its best
will you swear to protect your company's address book?
and believe in the people in it?
and help them realize their potential?
and sleep with some of them occasionally?

to crush the competition is the signifier of choice
in this abstract sunny afternoon
and there is potential
if we are to stick to
well-understood gestures

phase ii

now assume a role
and shop for an angry chihuahua
the self should go — on principle —
for rum-and-coke
so the script doesn't suffer
from scholarly neglect
a requiem for sustained engineering efforts
the tyranny of inescapable affinities
halfway through the corporate sponsor speech
it became obvious that our job
is more like paraphrasing than
to engineer the human soul

let there be criterion other than class:
inside every human a God
hidden under an umbrella
to drive the ghosts away from
the reality established earlier
and waiting for the puzzle to
get easier: publicly displaying
affection to get through the ceiling
without expectations
I am aesthetically exhausted
my death suits the taste
of political analysts
keep eye contact all the time
language is the worst place to host desire

the workings of desire
working with desire
anything to solve the moonshine
murder case: baby steps
microwave things in batches:
a proven methodology for mingling
while advertising the town to the brokers

keep your desires
until the winter where most animals
are asleep and only humans
are walking around with laptops
and dreams of proper hierarchies of production

phase iii

done forced feeding
this whip-lashed destiny
this jarred teabag
screaming "too small
give me a darkroom
without visible service lines"

to set softly your breakthroughs
as birthday gifts
traditionally, the library
system can be opposed
one reboot at a time

tattooed in increments
side effect backstabbing
comes with collision
and hip damage

arcade astronauts sale
tough luck
printing the friendly asphalt after 7:00
leave me alone in suburbia:
for redemption of
oil deathbed arabia
serenading backward
with pagan-ish ceilings

my first advice is measure measure measure
before giving someone a lift
I googled you but
I stayed in isolation
and was granted a second chance
to arrange my action heroes in alphabetic order
a brotherhood landed in my lap

not breaking the gestures code now
yet exploring all other encrypted alternatives
so much for the end of the season stunt
I won't use the shredding machine
sweetened secondhand traps
what if passion is falling behind
scripted suburbia honeymoon dragging its feet
one web page after another
a superb extravaganza of arabic numerals

my software is your wound
day-in day-out in this
astonishing aerodynamics
but yet to find an angel from the
quality control staff

I'm gonna exercise my semantic rights here: e.g.
taking hope out of the equation using direct substitution
coz who is trained to agree by default
home is such a nagging concept
and a matter of laying out definitions

without expecting the future to happen anytime soon
I am talking pragmatics here:
one tongue to lick the absolute and the other
is to keep track of the 520 traffic jam

you suckers for scientific evolution
God is yet to be discovered as a question of efficacy
assuming that something will eventually happen
we can still imagine an erotic trip
download your objects of affections beforehand
I'm slowly starting
a new trend of broken promises
first: the invisible river name
second: I forgot my
key in the door thinking that a
great banking experience
is what I need today
but awareness freaks me out
and destiny is a collage item
to hold against the yard sale in the background
camera flood creation
oh, nothing but symptoms
agency of static poses
an ontological evidence is not a place for hobbyists
customer service closed evenings and weekends
in the editing phase I realized: I won't ever find you
but art has visitation rights too

bathrooms are only for citizens
and for your spiritual beauty: a vision
distanced from oil
knocked one two three threats down
memory borrowed not printed
stop europe from starting
this cream puff corner shop
and grow more coordinated limbs
setting sleep aside, only few challenges are left

to enter speechless the emergency queue
the dry signifiers walk in
a city afraid to forget you
but not as much as the olympics theme
maybe to honor the market edge
there is clapping downtown — did you forget
the hundred forms of intimacy?
the disk jockey spinning sulfur
resonance comes handy though
I thought I saw them I lived
to climb their memories
while tucked inside a mimetic sandwich
in this afternoon heat sleepwear kisses music
beware of the hammer
I'd be in love for two weeks
the trick is whatever was left out will eventually
bring more dualism for the money
a ramp hidden by the umbrella
said to drive the burden away

guess the gratitude waiting for one puzzle
to get easier that is another expression
for dashing through as things fall from
the ceiling

throw in the towel no offense taken
it is worth the time compaction
we're doing it for the fun that will
later be lamented no matter how astonishing
in its autonomous structure
left the conversation without clear outcome
a craft so magical I admired its
loneliness we started the office strike walking
the pop songs are far from remembered
but the good view sometimes arrives early
unless it's wrecked by forward movements
under the crowded
scene "no comment" the officer said all evening
in history searching for a mate

phase iv

< start of phase iv / >
< middle of phase iv / >
< end of phase iv / >

phase v

< autonomy / >

    or

< if yes, goto phase X / >
< if no, go . . . / >

    or

There was little to do

There was little to do about the health of the organization
So they handed each one cleaner genitals
Then discussed for hours the immigration policies
It was possible again to find love
At least this was the rumor:
Social networking, Web 2.0, etc . . .
More ways to communicate our desires to the entrepreneurs
The ones John the Baptist hallucinated about
Dragging their mute music to forgiving cities
In the organic market healthy professionals eating healthy food
The owner of the flood occupied the third floor of the fan club
And the only thought in his head was "cheap desires cheap
        migration capital"
We were supposed to do creative things today
So we passed by a rocket
It was so cold when we decided to calm the fuck down
And when I asked the drama teacher about God, I admit,
I was into saving myself
So I needed moments of greatness
Oh thank you again for the first kiss Mr. assassin
The poem I failed to write is chasing me
The poets I left in the balcony to dry stayed wet
Now I smell like sweat except that I have my sexy laptop
I'm a good slave and I am happy today

Under the sign of efficiency

Under the sign of efficiency
I had my flag
And a universe to back it up
I often mistook its cleanliness for causality
The hood, the world, I have every right to be hungry tonight
Albeit they were changing the world outside my office
Using the sunshine repair kit
We were climbing the terrains of hope
And looked at the CTO's brain
And we all agreed: "here is a man who truly loves himself"

The business of resentment

In graduate school we became what we studied
In the background a sad machine gun went off
"it was supposed to be a quick in & out operation"
The freedom fighters prayed to the machine gun God
My friend called me three times before dawn: "how
does it feel to be this sad?"
I made a phone call to measure your love
Suddenly we woke up from the dreams software
brings to our reasonable beings

Text messages

1

What a sad story
Picking a fight
In this desolate strip club
May arrogance save you brother
From the dull competition
By the ATM machine

2

We were split into third and first worlds
There was sand, grant applications
Movies, and poems to describe our differences
And we had little free time
Because we were all business during the day
"Infinite number of mountain tops for your viewing
        pleasure"
Here is a world of good management practice
Take my blood tonight, taste it, like in Christianity
Ah, lucky us, never having to escape what we were told
        to believe
I'm not gonna hit on the waitress
I will ask 3rd world poets to read slowly
If you translate them they'll have sex with you
Yeah, colonialism is my poetic strategy
Did you get my voice message yet?

Almost, I guess, but I'm not good at holding back
Especially after you demonstrated that you're my buddy

3

Waking up every morning in fear
Of the market passing by
It is so scary to age in a capitalist world
Some of us got to define money
Some got to juggle art and life
Decide at which point to sell out
The pear looks like a man's testicle
I'm getting a life in a car

4

This can't be the world
Dancing as substitute for
Reality: start the dance early
A home falling on the passengers
We can only believe with broken egos
I can only believe in this moon surrendering
To a one night stand with itself
It is the world beneath us
that has sadness all around
The VP of research and development is around
So watch your words buddy
And cut corners on your way back, it is war war
and all beginners left at 11:30

5

We kept a distance from the music
Our happiness was built on others
Think of it, it is a two way street
Have you listened to my voice message yet?
I'm the master magician of this primitive tribe
"Yale and Harvard deployments are superior
To Michigan State or Cornell"
A heart broken with excellence
This is my baby, this is the awareness it brings
No one twists the arms of a stranger
Give me more money yo
We'll handle this drama with care if
We second guessed ourselves
You, vocal priest, take a moment out of the suburbs
You knew me a genius of ceramic placement
We are the white race, the alpha and the enthusiasm

6

The Seattle skyline is clear
And I want to write
Poems about humans
How our love is pure
And how we never believe in
One theory:
Some of us are listening
— Arrogant and driven —
To the sound of things alive

7

The body: a simplification

We were text messaging across
The street, we were also in the middle of the
Majestic opera house
The car race is over with its ambiguous rules
And It triggered all hidden class issues

Now it is all about how we saw the world or how we opposed
Or didn't oppose evil
Hoping for an absolute to bring
The semantic to conclusion, you dig?

8

One extra story circulating
Among the witnesses
It is a human town
That I'm roaming tonight
These men are silly
I'm leaving town
Looking for a different kind of guilt
Why do I still exist in my poems?
The stunt man is grounded for the night
Sipping straight scotch in front
Of his lover's mirrors
And I'm losing all my friends to pragmatism

9

I was in that helicopter
Practicing my golf swing
When the therapist decided
Cut off the alcohol son
I said fuck you fuck
Your family dear therapist
Here is a shot at dysfunctionality
We argued often, and this is how much it hurts

10

Inspecting the saints

They hid wisdom
I brought the sea over for confession
Ah, all this business of moving in . . .
All this decadence
You brought the sea over for two minutes
The mountain isn't as social
And without sins, so you brought the sea
The trouble with wisdom is its uselessness
The beauty of uselessness is its lack of wisdom
You're not that charming without her
You're just crazy, yet comfortable in your madness
Okay, let us pick up the moon
And fuck it in a moving car
Have you listened to my voice message yet?

I'm hiding my question marks for the first week
Do you get it, do you get the dream behind the dance
Let the music be poetry poverty violence
Now you deserve a poem
When all is said and done, it is not that hard to find a place
to cheat on your lover
It is seemingly a random city, a random chore
Do you believe we will end up there soon?
Without judgment, without a city
Did you cut my lips?
Was the meaning too ridiculous to build a city on?
I'll drive you crazy sometimes
But you still love me, don't you?

11

Elizabeth was there
All her sentences were sexy and grey
With wind that hurts your emotions
I look at you O wonderful bridge
And ask, how did you believe in reality
The stranger is tired
Our friends were hooked to communication devices
They stepped out of surrealism
For a second or two
Do you believe me?
I have it all here, especially its sound

12

Bad-ass Pakistanis dancing salsa

They say, you're my only celebrity
Your majesty I don't get the rhythm
I'm alone in this algorithm
So much tension in the cable
Retaining our suave employees is a priority
You guys listen to the music
Something irresponsible in the music
Dancing with your skirt off
I hear you brothers and sisters

13

Is it a signal we're dead
In a simple field trip
My modest life extended
By movies and stuff
I want to call all of you
Crime story buffs or
Creatures of habit,
Dope, and Xbox games
Million boxes of death
Gifts and turbines make for
Our tough business plan

14

Death is just another tool for the living to use
In the pursuit of happiness
Soccer is such a beautiful sport, with all
The time spent driving around
I see my shadow fades:
It is one more thing to sacrifice for meaning?
So many things are over the world also is over

15

A resurrection plan
So longing to make sense
As long as the movie is not over
I have these dreams and issues
I am over the movie
Plot and its structure
A drum interferes
Savoring the narrative deal
We get famous
We drive slowly
Get our act together
Home sweet home
How old are you?
And is it enough to log into my system
Have you listened to my voice message yet?
I abhor this poem's face
What was your profit margin today?

16

Don't scream, the movie isn't that scary
You just lost a little bit of freedom today
Buy this view in the city
How much do you need to stay alive?
Probably not much, a home or two
My image is in the streets of Cairo
Bare foot and with an American flag in my mind
You my friend are the real deal

Arabs in search of news

DC Opens: Arabs in search of news
Midnight is rarely offered here
It is only forced against this information lust
I'm too in search of information
And not just these sudden belief systems
I encountered on the tips of the airplane wings
I'll go down while thinking irrelevant thoughts
Yet I will be thinking them deeply
You must be from Seattle to be able to do so
Yes, I'm also from Arabia, we travel on the backs
Of well-fed camels: tick tick tick without dreams
Or ethnocentric political thoughts: derivatives derivatives
Whose escape plan is this?
Call it dignity if you like, but sort it out, and remember
You don't stand a single chance against cuteness
From each according to his abilities
And to each according to his sugar mama's love
Oh liquid email we drink you in the morning we drink you
In the afternoon, we drink and we drink
And we throw a finger licking pose at the end
Purple strategist of the after world,
There are simple descriptions of everything
And once mastered the world will feel safer
Even with murder to wear in the future
Our friends really cared, they just waited
For cheaper and sexier mobile devices to call us from

These were times made not to risk reasoning
How did they figure out that we are easy to hustle?
Please smile, the airport security is watching
They mistook the meanings of these ink scribbles
Yes we were lost and the earth isn't to take us kindly
Sugar mama please forsake us
What if we die strangers?
Life is taking us to the chess boards
But remember, as a manager, your role
Is to think about velocity: theirs and ours
We are always alive for a couple of days
Being self critical doesn't always work
And you should be coy about it: No more
Surrealist interviewing skills, just average
            management please

One card poem/mirror

Enormous labyrinth positioned off the main street

> Skinny soul worker
> You must be kidding
> I'm yours in simple cases only
> Let us take a chance
> Golfing for God or synchronized swimming
>   for Yahweh
> Each four years in the Olympics
> We go to the town square and play soccer
> With the president's guards

We say that we're here for the music and not for parking
All the dogs in late capitalism garden say the truth
Like: "I know you're cute"
& "Yes, they're killing Arabs all over"
But we communicate more efficiently "you're so cute,
    you know"
I won't be able to shake your hand if you have a grenade
    in the other one
"war works hard" & there isn't time to understand

What if we offended your employees

1

What if we offended your employees?
Suddenly they turned away from the spaceship
"officer on board" people screamed
Father father my tummy hurts
People loved to come by and utter their will:
       "I grant you my most significant desire . . ."

2

The angry people around here declared the train station
       a no-fly zone
The rest of us were accused of being ethnically agreeable
And always under self-imposed discipline
There are moments of forgetfulness
While filling out immigration petitions
Listening to the mechanics of desire making the news
So, don't think ill of freedom
I just want to smell this sentence

3

What language do you do business in?
This landscape was once offered to Eros
And he declined it citing lack of ambition
Later he ventured in Persian carpets and bridging
        intellect and passion
I wasn't sure what to do then with the love poems
        I inherited
My friend said "no worries, I will get you a date
With the zoo's CIO"
She likes poetry, and she won't test your character
Yet give you plenty of coupons

Touch my history lightly,
touch the stray desert

Touch my history lightly, touch the stray desert

- + yesterday I was around
- + tomorrow wasn't in the future, this system of signs will die tomorrow, it will flower, it will wake our town — but we have you where we want you: scared and driving to the end of the block
- + Are you okay?
- + I'm okay, leave me your American dream. It rains in Seattle, it rains in my apartment, it rains in America and the people outside are either smoking or checking their voice mails "love me, it's war time, yes"
- + The actor said the bar is closing in 15 minutes:
- + This pride is over-priced
- + Why park in the designated spot, if you can simply crash into something
- + Here is a letter: I see your job as a verb,
      As a possible conversation starter

I'm your mothering equipment except that I'll leave early
What a lousy grammar?
        It is in my nature
        You can crash here tonight
        You have the worst possible timing

MAGED ZAHER was born and raised in Cairo, Egypt, where he earned an M.Sc. degree in structural engineering, specializing in computer aided design. In 1995, he led the team that did the analysis of the seismic effect on the Meridian high rise hotel in Giza, Egypt. In 1998 he earned a master's degree in computer science from the University of Akron, Ohio. He has worked at many large software companies, and participated in building products such as AutoCad, Hotmail, Windows Presentation Foundations, and Microsoft Student. His main areas of interest are API (Application Programming Interface) design and building scalable and flexible SOA (Service Oriented Architecture) systems.